Run and Hike,
Play and Bike

to Mrs. Tama, my sixth-grade and eighth-grade teacher in Rocky River, Ohio
—B.P.C.

to Ms. Stipanicic, keep moving!
—M.G.

Physical Activity:
Movement of the body in a way that uses energy

Run and Hike, Play and Bike

What Is Physical Activity?

by Brian P. Cleary

illustrations by Martin Goneau

consultant Jennifer K. Nelson, Master of Science,
Registered Dietitian, Licensed Dietitian

M Millbrook Press • Minneapolis

Physical activity
occurs when you're in motion,

whether you are jumping rope

or swimming in the ocean.

Your body's using energy

with each and
every movement,

and all of this activity can lead to health improvement.

(except their thumbs and fingers
on their keyboard or remote).

TVs and computers?
There's nothing wrong with either.

But when it comes to exercise,

you'll find that it's in neither.

Experts say that kids should try to spend about an hour

every day in exercise
to help build muscle power.

Moving keeps you flexible.
It plays a crucial part

in strengthening your bones and lungs
and pumping up your heart.

Do you enjoy activities like shooting hoops or hiking?

Playing catch or hopscotch,

perhaps a lazy jog,

mowing lawns or playing fetch or Frisbee with your dog-

will make it so, although you sweat,

you're able to keep talking.

Exercise that's vigorous
is done at faster paces,

like swimming hard, aerobics, and both foot and cycle races.

These all boost your heart rate.
They help in burning fat.

They increase your endurance and do even more than that.

Physical activity
can make us feel less

anxious,

cooped up,

wound up,

  strained,

or tense with
lots of stress.

And so when mapping out your day, there's no need to be quizzical:

a healthy day's a happy day,

so make time to be physical!

So what is physical activity? Do you know?

You should aim for at least 60 minutes of moderate or vigorous physical activity every day or most days. Get an adult to join you—adults need at least 30 minutes each day. Go to www.MyPyramid.gov to learn how being active is part of being healthy.

Kick around a soccer ball (or any ball)!

Rake leaves into a pile—
then jump in it!

Practice martial arts!

Go in-line skating around
the neighborhood!

Grab some friends for a
game of tag or tug-of-war!

This book provides general information about physical activity in accordance with the MyPyramid guidelines created by the United States Department of Agriculture (USDA). The information in this book is not intended as medical advice. Anyone with certain health conditions, including food allergies or sensitivities, asthma, diabetes, heart disease, or high blood pressure, should follow the advice of a physician or other medical professional.

Find activities, games, and more at
www.brianpcleary.com

ABOUT THE AUTHOR, ILLUSTRATOR & CONSULTANT

BRIAN P. CLEARY is the author of the Words Are CATegorical®, Math Is CATegorical®, Adventures in Memory™, Sounds Like Reading®, and Food Is CATegorical™ series, as well as several picture books and poetry books. He lives in Cleveland, Ohio.

MARTIN GONEAU is the illustrator of the Food Is CATegorical™ series. He lives in Trois-Rivières, Québec.

JENNIFER K. NELSON is Director of Clinical Dietetics and Associate Professor in Nutrition at Mayo Clinic in Rochester, Minnesota. She is also a Specialty Medical Editor for nutrition and healthy eating content for MayoClinic.com.

Millbrook Press
A division of Lerner Publishing Group, Inc.
241 First Avenue North
Minneapolis, MN 55401 U.S.A.

Website address: www.lernerbooks.com

Library of Congress Cataloging-in-Publication Data

Cleary, Brian P., 1959–
    Run and hike, play and bike : what is physical activity? / by Brian P. Cleary ; illustrations by Martin Goneau ; consultant Jennifer K. Nelson.
        p.   cm. — (Food is CATegorical)
    ISBN: 978-1-58013-593-1 (lib. bdg. : alk. paper)
    1. Exercise—Juvenile literature. I. Goneau, Martin, ill. II. Title.
QP301.C5854 2011
612.7'6—dc22   2009046353

Manufactured in the United States of America
1 – PC – 7/15/10